Kings and Queens of East Africa

Sylviane Anna Diouf

Watts LIBRARY

Franklin Watts
A Division of Grolier Publishing
New York • London • Hong Kong • Sydney
Danbury, Connecticut

Note to readers: Definitions for words in **bold** can be found in the Glossary at the back of this book.

Cover illustration by Gary Overacre, interpreted from a photograph by © Corbis-Bettmann

Photographs ©: Art Resource, NY: 40 (Giraudon); BBC Natural History Unit: 3 bottom, 34 (Sarah Byatt); Bridgeman Art Library International Ltd., London/New York: 24, 25 (STC67046/Grand Portico of the Temple of Philae, Nubia, from "Egypt and Nubia", Vol.1, by David Roberts. 1838. Colour lithograph. Stapleton Collection, UK), 26 (AMQ114262/Jar decorated with lion masks and cobra goddesses on lotus flowers, from Tomb 1090. Faras, Sudan, 1st-2nd century AD. Painted pottery. Height: 19.3 cm. Ashmolean Museum, Oxford, UK); Corbis-Bettmann: 23 (Chris Hellier), 21 (Charles & Josette Lenars), 15, 44; Culver Pictures: 50; Gerald Cubitt: 48; Liaison Agency, Inc.: 12 (P. Bronstein), 36 (Alexis Duclos), 20 (Hulton Getty), 31 (Reza), 28 (Roger-Viollet); Mary Evans Picture Library: 29 (Illustrated London News, 10 May, 1884), 51 (ILN), 46 (Journal des Voyages vol 23), 3 top, 47 (Le Petit Journal), 22 (Le Petit Journal, 1901), 14, 17, 30; National Geographic Image Collection: 8, 9 (Garrett, Kenneth and Leakey Meave); Panos Pictures: 27 (Sean Sprague); Photo Researchers: 52, 53 (Georg Gerster); Stock Montage, Inc.: 16, 19, 33, 42; Superstock, Inc.: 6, 10, 38, 39, 49.

Maps by XNR Productions.

Visit Franklin Watts on the Internet at:
http://publishing.grolier.com

Library of Congress Cataloging-in-Publication Data

Diouf, Sylviane Anna
    Kings and queens of East Africa / by Sylviane Anna Diouf
       p.   cm.— (Watts Library)
    Includes bibliographical references and index.
    Summary: A survey of the historical regions and kingdoms of East Africa, including biographies of Ranavalona I, Queen of Madagascar; Yambio, King of the Azande; and Menelik II, Emperor of Ethiopia.
    ISBN 0-531-20373-5 (lib. bdg.)   0-531-16534-5 (pbk.)
    1. Africa, Eastern—Kings and rulers—Biography—Juvenile literature. 2. Africa, Eastern—History—Juvenile literature. [1. Africa, Eastern—Kings and rulers. 2. Kings, queens, rulers, etc. 3. Africa, Eastern—History.] I. Title. II. Series.
DT365.47.K36 2000
967.6'01'0922—dc21
                                            99-086637

Contents

Legend

- The Realm of Ranavalona
- The Azande Kingdom
- The Ethiopian Empire

- Modern national boundary
- ⊛ Modern capital city

SUDAN

Khartoum ⊛

White Nile R.

Blue Nile R.

Asmara ⊛

ERITREA

Lake Tana

DJIBOUTI ⊛ Djibouti

⊛ Addis Ababa

ETHIOPIA

SOMALIA

CENTRAL
AFRICAN
REPUBLIC

*Lake Turkana
(Lake Rudolf)*

UGANDA

Kampala ⊛

KENYA

⊛ Nairobi

Mogadishu ⊛

RWANDA

⊛ Kigali

*Lake
Victoria*

▲ Mt.
Kilimanjaro

DEMOCRATIC
REPUBLIC
OF THE
CONGO

⊛ Bujumbura

BURUNDI

Lake Tanganyika

TANZANIA

Dar es Salaam ⊛

*Indian
Ocean*

MALAWI *Lake Malawi
(Lake Nyasa)*

Lilongwe ⊛

ZAMBIA

Lusaka ⊛

Zambezi R.

MOZAMBIQUE

Harare ⊛

ZIMBABWE

MADAGASCAR

⊛ Antananarivo

BOTSWANA

SWAZILAND

Maputo ⊛

LESOTHO

AFRICA

Area
enlarged

*Atlantic
Ocean*

*Indian
Ocean*

N

0   500

0   500 km

Chapter One

Kings and Queens of Africa

Africa is a continent of great natural diversity—burning deserts, snowy mountains, lush forests, dry savannas, and majestic rivers. Africa's 800 million people are as diverse as its landscape. Thousands of different populations live in the continent's fifty-three countries. Africans speak 25 percent of the 6,000 languages that exist on Earth.

For tens of thousands of years, Africans have shared the beauty of this vast continent. The peoples used Africa's immense resources while each population developed its own culture, language, and traditions. This amazing diversity could be a source of richness or of division, but from the earliest times Africa has had great leaders who united diverse communities into strong nations.

The kings and queens of Africa were concerned not only with power and the expansion of their kingdoms but also with justice, education, arts, crafts, agriculture, and trade. Some ruled in difficult times. The arrival of the Europeans, the rise of the slave trade, and colonization unsettled their territories and the entire continent. The rulers faced external threats and internal divisions, and they had to invent ways to govern and protect their communities.

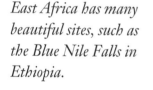

East Africa has many beautiful sites, such as the Blue Nile Falls in Ethiopia.

Accounts of the kings and queens of Africa have been passed from one generation to the next through stories and songs. Starting in the eighth century, travelers from North Africa recorded their observations of African rulers in books and letters. Africans, writing in Arabic, did the same, starting in the 1500s. Europeans first arrived in Africa in 1944, and they left records of the rulers and the courts they visited. Both natives and foreigners have helped us know the rulers who, with their people, have created the history of Africa.

For the series, *Kings and Queens of Africa*, the continent has been divided into four parts: West, Central, Southern, and East. Each area has characteristics that helped to shape the cultures that developed there. West Africa was a crossroads for trade, and kingdoms and empires based largely on commerce rose in this region. Central Africa was transformed by the migration of the Bantu population from the northwest. East Africa was molded by the great variety of its peoples. Large movements of population changed the course of Southern Africa's history.

Each book in this series looks at different eras to show how the region evolved through time and the most significant rulers of the region. Some were more famous than others, and some well-known figures do not appear here. I have presented social, political, and cultural innovators who connected their kingdoms to a larger world, defended their territory against foreign invasions, or brought various groups together into one people. These rulers left important legacies.

An experienced fossil finder searches the rock-strewn landscape of East Africa for remains of early human life.

Chapter Two

The Kingdoms of East Africa

East Africa is characterized by great variety in peoples, cultures, and religions. Bantu, Arabs from North Africa and the Middle East, **Nilotic** people, black Hebrews, **Indonesians**, and others have lived here for centuries. This area is often called the cradle of humankind because the earliest evidence of human life has been found in its valleys.

Great kingdoms have emerged here. The most ancient flourished in Nubia, in the Sudan, 5,000 years ago. Although the

Sudan is often considered part of North Africa, geographically and historically it belongs more closely to East Africa. Christian kingdoms prospered in the Sudan and Ethiopia 1,700 years ago, and Muslim kingdoms developed later. In Zimbabwe, the Great Zimbabwe culture of about 1000 to 1450 left a large, impressive city of stone.

An Afro-Asian Kingdom

Among the kingdoms that rose in East Africa was Great Zimbabwe, known today from the ruins of its magnificent stone buildings.

Madagascar symbolizes the diversity of the region. This island's population is a mix of Africans from the continent and Indonesians who sailed to the "Big Island" centuries ago. By the sixteenth century, the ethnic groups that make up the **Malagasy** people were living in small kingdoms. Soon, Arabians, Portuguese, Dutch, British, and French began sending Malagasy slaves to the Middle East and the West Indies.

By the early nineteenth century, the Merina kingdom had emerged as the most powerful state. Its queen, Ranavalona I (c. 1788–1861), tried to modernize her country and open it to international trade while resisting the French and British who wanted control of the island.

The Many Fights of the Azande

The Azande, who entered southern Sudan in the eighteenth century, were warriors who subdued several populations and created a powerful state. When Yambio (c. 1835–1905) became their leader, the region was in turmoil. The Azande were preyed on by local peoples and foreigners including the Egyptians, Muslim revolutionaries, British, Belgians, and French.

The Azande kingdom of Sudan was short-lived. Still, its determined ruler, King Yambio, symbolizes the struggle of many African leaders and peoples to remain independent.

Old and New Ethiopia

Ethiopia has a long history of powerful empires, starting twenty-three centuries ago in Aksum. Later, Christian and Muslim kingdoms appeared. Their brilliant cultures left monuments and written testimonies of their accomplishments.

In the nineteenth century, the kingdoms of Ethiopia united in a strong empire led by Theodoros II and his successor, Yohannes IV. Menelik II (1844–1913), who assumed power in 1889, continued the policy of consolidation and led a powerful empire. He and his wife, Empress Taytu (1840–1918), adopted those foreign elements they thought were useful, while protecting the traditions and independence of their land. Under Menelik II's leadership, Ethiopia remained a free country, escaping the colonization that plagued the rest of the continent.

This boy is standing on a small section of Madagascar's 3,000 miles (4,828 km) of coastline.

Chapter Three

Ranavalona I, Queen of Madagascar

On July 27, 1828, King Radama I died at the age of thirty-six. In his short life, he had united almost all the groups and clans of the island of Madagascar into one kingdom. He introduced Christian missionaries and craftsmen, and he opened his country to outside influences. After his death, the question of who would rule next was hotly contested. In the end,

The Lost Island

Madagascar broke off from Africa 165 million years ago. Over the next 45 million years, it slowly drifted to its present location.

his wife, Ranavalona, who was also his cousin, was selected. She was crowned Ranavalona I.

The Big Island

Ranavalona's country was a vast island, the fourth-largest in the world, with beautiful landscapes of green hills and a diverse population. The "Big Island," as it is sometimes called, was settled around A.D. 500 by people who arrived in boats. Some came from Africa, 250 miles (400 km) to the west, and some came from as far as Indonesia, 4,000 miles (6,436 km) away. By the eleventh century, the island people were actively trading with Arabs who had settled along the east coast of Africa.

Radama I ruled Madagascar from 1810 to 1828.

The people of the island are called Malagasy. They speak several languages that are derived from Indonesian and include words from African languages and Arabic. The principal language is Merina.

Queen Ranavalona

King Radama left a unified kingdom. But Queen Ranavalona had different political and religious ideas.

14

Merina

Merina means "those from the country where one can see far," a reference to the highlands the Merina people inhabit. When they entered the central highlands of Madagascar the Merina found people called *vazimba* (ancestors), who were descended from Bantu and early Indonesian settlers. Under King Andrianampoinimerina, the Merina strengthened their kingdom and unified several non-Merina states. After his death, his son Radama I continued the unification of the island. The Merina are the largest ethnic group in Madagascar. The illustrator shows a village in Madagascar in the early nineteenth century.

When she came to the throne, she surrounded herself with the people her husband had avoided, and she ordered her rivals killed.

The queen's first concern was to keep her kingdom independent and to protect it from the influence of the European

*The illustration shows
Queen Ranavalona I,
ruler of Madagascar,
in1845.*

powers—especially Great Britain and France, which occupied
nearby islands in the Indian Ocean. She told the British that
she would not honor a treaty they had made with her husband.
She stopped trade between Madagascar and the island of Mauritius, controlled by the British, and Réunion, controlled by
the French.

In 1829, after a number of arguments with the queen, King Charles X of France ordered his forces to invade the cities of Tamatave and Tintingue. But he had not counted on the determination and national pride of the Malagasy and their queen. The French were defeated and had to retreat.

Ranavalona's fear of foreign influence was not just political: she did not want the Malagasy to turn away from their traditional religion to embrace Christianity. In his time, King Radama I welcomed Anglican missionaries, who made a few converts, and Protestantism began to spread. Ranavalona saw Christianity as a threat to the culture and traditions of the Malagasy.

One day, in 1835, Ranavalona assembled the missionaries and said, "I tell you plainly that I will oppose any

This drawing shows a nineteenth-century soldier of Madagascar. Ranavalona depended upon her forces.

Religions

More than 50 percent of the Malagasy follow a traditional religion. Their god is called *Zanabary* (the Creator), or *Andriamanita* (Sweet Lord). About 20 percent of the Malagasy are Catholics, 20 percent are Protestants, and 7 percent are Muslim.

attempt by my people to change the customs of my ancestors . . . and with respect to religious worship . . . baptisms and [religious] societies, I forbid my people to take part." Nevertheless, she wanted the foreign missionaries to stay so that they could give the children a nonreligious education. "If you have new crafts or knowledge," she said, "to teach for the good of my people, do that, for it is good." The missionaries refused and were forced to leave. After their departure, their converts among the Malagasy were persecuted, and many were killed.

The Modernization of Madagascar

Although she opposed foreign influence, Queen Ranavalona was eager to modernize her country and to trade with the European powers. She wanted to import European goods and export the island's abundant rice and cattle. So in 1836, she sent a delegation to Paris and London to negotiate trade agreements and friendship treaties. The mission ended in failure. Madagascar did not sign treaties with either France or Britain.

The queen's insistence on independence angered the French and the British. In 1845, they sent a joint force to attack the island. Once again, Ranavalona's army defeated the foreigners. Soon afterward, the queen expelled the European traders and stopped all exports of rice and beef to Réunion and Mauritius.

Although European trade was ended, the queen maintained commerce with the United States. She decided that her

This 1858 drawing shows a royal procession to Antananarivo, the capital city of Madagascar.

people could produce some of the goods they had once imported. In a short time, factories employing more than 20,000 workers were in operation. They produced soap, glass, bricks, cement, ink, porcelain, rum, silk, guns, ammunition, and even cannons. Using their products, the queen had a large, beautiful palace erected in her capital, Antananarivo. Her scholars created the first dictionary of Merina and wrote a code of law. Queen Ranavalona continued her late husband's conquests and finally reigned over all the island.

The City of Antananarivo

Founded in the mid-seventeenth century by the Merina, Antananarivo means "the city of the thousand warriors."

Rakota, the crown prince of Madagascar in 1812. He reigned as King Radama II (1861–63), after his mother, Ranavalona I, died.

Ranavalona Betrayed

Meanwhile, the French and British were preparing new strategies to gain control. First, they offered a gesture of goodwill. In 1853, the traders of Mauritius and Réunion gave the queen $15,000 to compensate for the damages caused by their failed invasion in 1845. Trade was reestablished, and the British government sent Ranavalona a friendly letter. By 1857, relations seemed to be warming, but the two powers did not trust her and were following a careful plan. They knew that the queen's son, twenty-seven-year-old Rakoto Radama, was friendly toward foreigners and Christianity. So they plotted to overthrow the queen and replace her with her son. Rakoto, eager to rule, joined in the plan. But the conspiracy was discovered.

The queen spent the last years of her life traveling and living in her palace in Antananarivo.

Ranavalona was deeply hurt by her son's disloyalty. She had fought all her life against foreigners and rivals within the royal family. Now she found she could not trust even her son.

The last years of Ranavalona's life were spent traveling throughout the island and watching her favorite game—fights between bulls. On July 16, 1861, Queen Ranavalona died. Following tradition, 25,000 cattle were slaughtered during her funeral.

The Queen's Legacy

Despite his disloyalty, the queen had named her son, Rakoto, as her successor. He abolished her policy

After the French took control of Madagascar in 1883, the last queen, Ranavalona III, left the country and lived in exile in Paris. A French newspaper published this picture and an article about her life in Paris.

of closing the country to foreigners. He asked the missionaries to come back, allowed Europeans to buy land, and granted privileges to foreign traders. Many of these measures were unpopular and the young king's reign was brief. He was assassinated in 1863, and his wife, Rasoherina, became queen. Queen Ranavalona II succeeded her. Madagascar had one final monarch, Queen Ranavalona III, who reigned until 1883, when France seized control of the island. For the last 55 years of the monarchy—except for two years—the Big Island was ruled by women.

The French and British present Ranavalona I as a cruel queen who oppressed her people. Many Malagasy agree that she was domineering and sometimes harsh, but to them, she represents devotion to Madagascar. She repelled two European invasions, developed local industry, encouraged education, and preserved traditions and religions.

Peoples of the Island

Each ethnic group on Madagascar has a name related to the area it lives in, or to its origins. The second-largest group, the Betsimisaraka, are the people who are "numerous and inseparable." The Antalaotra are "people of the sea," while the Antairomo are "people of the shore." The Antaifasy are the "people of the sand," and the Tanala are the "people of the forest." This man is wearing the traditional dress of the Antandroy people.

Sudan has seen the rise of many cultures and kingdoms for centuries before the Azande. The ancient state of Nubia was one of the earliest.

Chapter Four

Yambio, King of the Azande

Even as a young boy, Yambio, who would become the leader of the Azande people, led a turbulent life, full of challenges, disappointments, and struggles. He was born around 1835. From his early childhood, he had to fight—for himself, for his mother—against his father and his brothers.

The Court of King Bazingbi

Yambio's mother, Ngbiara, was a young captive who lived at the court of King Bazingbi. The king had given her as a slave to his wife. When Ngbiara was older, she entered into a relationship with the king. A son, Yambio, was born from their union. Following the custom, Ngbiara and Yambio were not considered slaves but were now part of the royal family. The young boy was a prince and equal to the king's other children.

King Bazingbi's land was located in the largest country in Africa, the Sudan. Some Azande people had settled there in the sixteenth century. They came from southeastern areas that are now part of the Congo and the Central African Republic.

In the eighteenth century, an Azande military aristocracy led by Yambio's ancestors moved into southern Sudan. The military imposed itself upon the Azande groups that had settled there earlier. As a result of this military move, Azande became the largest state in southern Sudan. The kingdoms that made up this well-organized state were ruled by princes, under the central authority of the king.

Bazingbi, Yambio's father, had several wives and many sons. One day, one of the king's sons died, and it was believed that Ngbiara, Yambio's mother, had killed him. She was accused of being a

Decorated with lion masks and cobra goddesses on lotus flowers, this jar was found in a first- to second-century tomb in Sudan. It was made by an early people of the region of the Azande.

witch and was condemned to death. Yambio pleaded for her cause, and in the end, she was not killed but sent into exile. Her son chose to go with her. King Bazingbi was furious. By speaking for his mother and leaving the court, the young prince had questioned his father's authority.

Now Yambio was thought of as the son of a servant and a witch, and it was known that his father was angry with him. He lost the easy life he had been accustomed to. Yambio remained in exile with his mother until two noblemen persuaded the king to pardon him.

These young Sudanese boys live in the Azande region.

Yambio Takes the Throne

When King Bazingbi died in 1869, Yambio inherited the title of chief and the kingdom administered by his late father. His brothers were given other kingdoms. Yambio was now in his thirties, with a copper skin, a mustache, and a beard. However, being the king of the Azande was not easy. There were jealous princes and intruding foreigners to deal with.

Since before Yambio's birth, part of the Sudan had been controlled by the Turkish and the Egyptians who had conquered the land in the 1820s. The Azande kingdom, however, was well defended by its 20,000-man army.

At first, the foreign forces that occupied the Sudan were interested mostly in ivory. When the foreigners discovered that the supply was not as large as they had thought, they

Ivory—a valuable item of trade—drew foreign attention to East Africa. An old photograph shows a colonial ivory-collecting point.

turned to the slave trade. They sent raiding expeditions all over the country to abduct men, women, and children and then sent them to Egypt and to the Middle East as slaves.

A convoy of slaves in the Sudan

Yambio a Prisoner

Yambio was determined to protect his people from being enslaved. By 1880, he united all the Azande kingdoms. Together, they defeated the Egyptian army. The Egyptians then tried to get rid of Yambio by a trick. They lured him to their camp with the promise of a truce and seized him. For two years, Yambio lived in captivity with two of his sons, humiliated and poorly treated. One son died in jail. When he was

The Mahdists

The founder of the Mahdist movement was Muhammad Ahmad al-Mahdi (1848–85). Islam teaches that when the world ends, a religious leader, or *mahdi*, will redeem faithful Muslims. In 1881, al-Mahdi claimed he was the mahdi and called his followers together to fight foreign rule. His army defeated the Egyptians and a British force. In the scene shown here, the British general Charles George Gordon is killed by Mahdists in 1885. They then took Khartoum and gained control of most of the country. Ahmad al-Mahdi established a strict Muslim state. He died in 1885, and his state was defeated in 1898 by an alliance of Egyptian and British

forces. The Sudan was governed by a joint British and Egyptian administration until the 1950s.

finally freed, after the Egyptians and the Turks were expelled by a Sudanese rebellion led by a group called the Mahdists, Yambio vowed he would never be imprisoned again.

When he returned to his kingdom in 1884, Yambio banished the Arab traders who were still living there and refused to provide slaves to the new Islamic government. For ten years, King Yambio enlarged and consolidated his kingdom. His aim was to unite the Azande so that they could resist the invaders and the slave dealers as one strong force.

Muslims and Christians

Christianity and Islam were introduced in Sudan in the Nubia region, "the country of gold." Nubia stretches along the Nile River from southern Egypt to northern Sudan. Nubia was the birthplace of several highly developed cultures and kingdoms as early as 4000 B.C. Christianity was brought to the region by Egyptian and Ethiopian missionaries. The Christian kingdoms of Nubia reached their peak in the tenth century, and Nubian Christians fought alongside the Europeans during the Crusades.

The first Muslims arrived in Lower Nubia after the Arabs had conquered Egypt in A.D. 640. They were traders and teachers who settled and married among the Nubians. The religion flourished in the fourteenth century, after the fall of the Christian kingdoms, which enabled Islam to penetrate into the interior.

Today the majority of the Sudanese, including the Nubians, are Muslims. The Muslim students shown here are studying at a Koranic school. Christianity and traditional religions are strong in the south.

Preparing for War

Meanwhile, the Muslim revolutionaries who had freed Yambio from the Egyptians were turning against him because he was refusing to cooperate with them. They sent a force to subdue him. Yambio dispatched three **emissaries** to meet them and tell them that if they came as friends, they should remain east of the Hu River and not try to go any further. However, unsure of their true intentions, he prepared for war. He mobilized his troops and those of his sons, and created three battalions of warriors.

He had acted wisely, because when his messengers returned, they told him that the Mahdists had not come as friends but had already crossed the river and were ready to attack. Yambio and his followers decided to withdraw, as a first move, leaving behind a battalion that fought the invaders for about a month. Then Yambio's sons and their armies arrived from distant provinces and pursued the Mahdists. Seeing the warriors approach, the Mahdists began to retreat. In the end, they left Yambio's realm and never came back.

Two years later, in 1899, the Mahdist state fell. But Yambio's problems were far from over. Other people had their eyes on Azandeland. Great Britain, France, and Italy were interested in the Sudan, and Belgium was trying to get a foothold in the southern area.

Azande Against the Colonial Powers

Yambio believed that the Azande had to unite to stop the invaders and maintain their independence. But the other chiefs wanted to choose a side. Some allied with the French, others with the British, and still others with the Italians.

During a conference in Berlin in 1884–85, the European powers had decided to stop fighting one another over Africa. Great Britain, France, Germany, Portugal, Spain, and Bel-

gium agreed to carve Africa up among themselves and to turn the ancient kingdoms into colonies.

By the end of the 1890s, the French had entered Azandeland, in what is now the Central African Republic. The Belgians were at its southern border, in the Congo, and the British—who had taken control of the Sudan in 1899—were approaching. Yambio's territory was the only independent Azande state left. The king was now alone, facing three European powers.

Representatives from fourteen countries met in Berlin from November 1884 to February 1885 to divide up Africa.

33

The Azande realm included desert, grasslands, and savanna. Here villagers collect water from a lake, using leather water skins.

Yambio believed the Belgians were more of an immediate danger than the other Europeans. He determined to play one country against the other. He thought that if he had good relations with the British, the Belgians would not attack his kingdom out of fear of Great Britain's retaliation. So he invited the British to set up a trading post. He thought that the British would not be interested in his offer. If they were, and they showed up, he was prepared to fight them.

In January 1903, the British, accepting Yambio's offer, sent a group of soldiers to his territory. The Azande warriors attacked and defeated the British column. A year later, another British troop was dispatched. It met the same fate.

Yambio Strikes First

A few months after this second victory, as the Belgians prepared an offensive against his kingdom, Yambio struck first. Leading 10,000 Azande warriors, he attacked a Belgian fort. He soon realized that his soldiers' weapons were no match for the Belgians' rifles. After a three-day siege, the Azande buried their dead and left. Having lost his best soldiers, Yambio was crushed, and the Azande were demoralized. They were surrounded by hostile forces with superior weapons.

Yambio did not even have time to reorganize his army before another threat appeared. The British, taking advantage of the weakness of the Azande state, marched toward Yambio's capital of Bilikiwe in January 1905. They were helped by some lesser kings who had resisted Yambio's leadership.

In Bilikiwe, Yambio realized that his forces would not be able to fend off the advancing troops, so he decided to welcome them. He sent one of his sons, Gangura, and several other young men to meet them, carrying gifts of maize and groundnuts. The next morning, the British forces arrived at Yambio's court. The king, however, had hidden in a secret

Bilikiwe

Yambio's capital, Bilikiwe, was located in southern Sudan, near what is now Zaire.

A Sudanese boy near his hut

place a few miles away. His son Gangura asked the Azande men who had gathered to meet the British to lay down their arms. But one man shouted, "Why should we lay down our weapons while the other side does not do the same?" A British soldier shot him dead. The Azande who had put down their arms took them up again. In the confusion that followed, some Azande were made prisoners. Many fled into the bush, including Gangura, who could not be found by a party that searched for him for two days.

Meanwhile, a prisoner led the British to Yambio's hiding place. As they approached, the king fired at them and killed one soldier. When the soldiers returned fire, Yambio was shot in the arm. He threw away his rifle and said that he could not fight any longer. But when the British soldiers came closer, he killed three of them with a gun he had hidden behind his back.

The End of a Kingdom

The wounded king was locked up in a hut. No one knows what happened next. Some say he refused to eat or drink and let himself die. Others believe that one of his grandsons, who had been allowed to visit him, murdered him. Yambio's wounds were not life-threatening, but within days of his capture, on February 10, 1905, King Yambio died. He had vowed, twenty-three years earlier, never again to live in a prison.

After Yambio's death, his kingdom was divided among his sons and put under the authority of the British. His capital, Bilikiwe, was renamed Yambio. But Yambio's death did not mark the end of Azande resistance. **Guerrilla warfare** against the British continued until the end of World War I in 1918.

King Yambio was a strong **nationalist** who fought valiantly for the unification and sovereignty of his people. He left a legacy of fierce independence and of strong loyalty to the culture and traditions passed on by generations of Azande.

Rulers of Ethiopia often enjoyed views of scenic mountains. Shown here are the Simien Mountains, in central Ethiopia.

Chapter Five

Menelik II, Emperor of Ethiopia

On August 19, 1844, Ijjigayyehu, a young woman who worked in the palace of King Sahle Sellasie in the kingdom of Shoa, Ethiopia, gave birth to a boy she named Sahle Maryam. The boy's father was the oldest prince of the kingdom, Haile Malakot.

An Ethiopian miniature painting illustrates the story of the meeting of Solomon and the Queen of Sheba.

The prince, who was only nineteen years old, reluctantly acknowledged the child and married Ijjigayyehu. Since it was now known that the baby was part of the royal family, King Sahle Sellasie renamed him Menelik. This was an honored name because Menelik I had founded the dynasty that had ruled Ethiopia for close to 3,000 years. In the tenth century B.C., his mother, Makeda, the famous Queen of Sheba, was said to have gone to Jerusalem to meet King Solomon. According to Ethiopian and other sources, from their encounter one son, Menelik, was born.

Young Menelik

Almost 3,000 years later, his namesake, the young Menelik, was leading a happy life in Ankober, the capital of Shoa, in the southern part of Ethiopia. The kingdom, along with a number of other small realms, was independent. Most of Ethiopia was under the central authority of Emperor Theodoros. Menelik, like his father's subjects and about half of the population of Ethiopia, was Christian. Most other Ethiopians were Muslim. There was also a small population called **Beta Israel**, made up of Jews.

In 1855, as Menelik entered his eleventh year, his privileged life ended. Emperor Theodoros decided to integrate Shoa into his empire, and he sent troops to invade the kingdom. Five days before the surrender of the Shoans, King Haile Malakot, who had succeeded his father as king, died. Emperor Theodoros took the late king's wife, Ijjigayyehu; their son, Menelik; and other young men to his imperial court as hostages. Menelik's life changed dramatically.

The Orthodox Church

Ethiopia's Orthodox Church is one of the oldest Christian congregations in the world. Christianity was established in A.D. 331 at the court of King Ezana at Aksum. From Judaism, the Ethiopian Church has retained certain practices, such as observing rules about clean and unclean food, using special ways to butcher animals, and Saturday worship. The church also absorbed elements of traditional religions. Today 40 to 50 percent of Ethiopians belong to the Orthodox Church, and about an equal number are Muslims.

Life in Exile

For ten years, Menelik lived at the emperor's court. There, among young nobles from other vanquished kingdoms, he was educated. He also learned to make war. He was part of the emperor's close circle and was well treated. Years later Menelik said that although Theodoros "killed my father and took me to his court, he always loved me as a son; he educated me with the greatest care, and almost showed for me greater affec-

A nineteenth-century drawing shows Emperor Theodoros of Ethiopia.

tion than for his own son." Theodoros trusted him and gave him his daughter, Alatash, in marriage. Nevertheless, Menelik wanted to return to Shoa.

In 1865, with his mother and a few other hostages, including Alula and Wele, two friends from the North, Menelik escaped from the palace and went back to Ankober. While at the court of Theodoros, Menelik had become ambitious. He wanted to become the next emperor, the "king of kings," and, indeed, Theodoros had promised him the throne.

However, when the old emperor died in 1868, another man succeeded him—Yohannes IV. Bitter but helpless, Menelik remained in Ankober. After a few confrontations with the new monarch, he learned to cooperate with the **ras**, as the Ethiopians call their king.

Making Plans to Rule

To make sure he would one day rule, Menelik began collecting huge quantities of money by selling ivory, ostrich feathers, gold, gum, wax, coffee, honey, and fur. He wanted to be able to buy modern weapons so that he could defeat any rivals. He also sought alliance with the northern kingdoms.

Yohannes IV did not trust Menelik. He tried to gain control of him by peaceful means. He feared that if Menelik allied with the northern kings, his own authority would be threatened. He pushed Menelik to marry a woman he thought would be his spy at Menelik's court and report back to him about her husband's plans.

Menelik II, king of Ethiopia

Languages

The first written language of Ethiopia was Ge'ez. Ge'ez evolved out of a language brought by the Sabeans (southwestern Arabians who settled in Ethiopia in the seventh century B.C.) and the native languages they found in their new land. The Bible and other religious documents were translated into Ge'ez in the fourth century. The spoken language died 500 years later. It was replaced by Amharic, the language of the Amhara people. Amharic, like English, is read from left to right, unlike other Semitic languages such as Hebrew and Arabic. It is the official language of Ethiopia.

The woman Yohannes selected was Taytu Betul, who was born in the 1840s. She came from the kingdom of Tigre and was the sister of Alula and Wele, the young men who had been hostages of Theodoros along with Menelik. Taytu Betul became Menelik's fourth wife on Easter Day, 1883, in the main church in Ankober.

Taytu was well educated. She could read and write in Amharic, the main language of Ethiopia. She liked poetry. She was an excellent chess player, a good cook, and a skilled weaver. Taytu was also a devout Christian. Her generosity to the church and respect for the priests were legendary. Contrary to what Yohannes IV had hoped, she was loyal to her husband and was a good influence on him.

Emperor of Ethiopia

When Emperor Yohannes IV died in a battle against Egypt in 1889, Menelik was ready. No one could challenge him. He had a strong political base, alliances with several kingdoms, and a large supply of arms. He proclaimed himself emperor of Ethiopia.

It was a time of political uncertainty when the European countries were scrambling to gain colonies in Africa. Emperor Menelik signed a treaty with Italy recognizing that country's seizure of a piece of land on the Red Sea known as Eritrea. The Italian officials prepared two versions of the treaty, one in Amharic and the other in Italian, but they were different. The Italian version made Ethiopia a subject state. When this was discovered, Menelik was furious. Empress Taytu declared that even though she disliked war, she was ready to fight. The Italians were confident that they could crush the empire by fanning the divisions between the emperor and his rivals. They invaded the province of Tigre in the northern part of Ethiopia.

Empress Taytu

Italy's Role

The Italians established themselves in the area of Eritrea (from the Latin *mare erythreum,* or "Red Sea") and gained recognition of its annexation by the Treaty of Wuchale in 1889. But when they invaded Tigre, they were defeated by Menelik.

In 1935, 500,000 Italians invaded Ethiopia. They killed 700,000 Ethiopians, burned thousands of churches, and destroyed houses and cattle. Emperor Haile Selassie appealed to the League of Nations (the international organization that preceded the United Nations), which did nothing to help. Encouraged by the world's indifference, Italy invaded the Sudan in 1940. Great Britain controlled that territory and pushed back the Italians. Ethiopia was finally liberated by the British and their African troops in 1941. After a long war with Ethiopia, which considered Eritrea one of its provinces, the country became independent in 1993.

This painting shows the battle in which the Ethiopian forces defeated an Italian invasion in 1896.

The ras of Tigre asked for the emperor's assistance, and Menelik called all Ethiopians to join him in defending their homeland. There was enthusiastic support. On March 1, 1896, at dawn, 18,000 Italian troops moved toward the Ethiopians' camp in Tigre. They hoped to surprise the Ethiopians at prayer. But sentinels alerted Menelik and Taytu. When the troops arrived, between 80,000 and 110,000 Ethiopians were ready. Within three hours, 6,000 invading soldiers had died, 1,500 were wounded, and 1,800 were prisoners. It

was a great victory for Menelik and Taytu, who had sent her own troops onto the battlefield.

A New Capital

Rid of the foreign menace, Menelik and the empress turned their attention to the modernization of Ethiopia. A few years before the war, Empress Taytu had made a beautiful valley her second home.

The valley was below the hill on which the capital, Entotto, was built. The climate was warmer. The valley was sheltered and had woods and warm springs. She called her retreat Addis Ababa, "the new flower." By 1889, Taytu's home became the capital of the empire. Empress Taytu financed the first hotel and helped to start an agricultural loan bank.

The crown of Emperor Menelik II

Addis Ababa, the capital of Ethiopia

The energetic Emperor Menelik II worked on many projects at the same time. His subjects could call on him whenever they needed. He was always curious and was fascinated by technology. He asked questions, wanting to know exactly how machines worked. He drove the first car in Addis Ababa.

The emperor was also an excellent administrator who set up the first national currency and an efficient tax system. To develop communications in his vast country, he created postal, telephone, and telegraph systems. Since Ethiopia lacked access to the sea, the emperor built a railroad line to link his capital to Djibouti, a foreign city on the Red Sea. With the railway, Ethiopia could send and receive goods from the harbor. Menelik and Taytu were both interested in education and the improvement of the Ethiopians' health, and they opened schools and hospitals. At Taytu's insistence, schools were planned for both boys and girls.

An Aging Ruler

Menelik II, seen at the end of his reign, ruled from 1889–1913, and he established the nation's independence from Italy.

All these activities took a toll on the emperor. In 1906, Menelik suffered a stroke. Gradually, he weakened and Empress Taytu took control as **regent**. She did not have children, and she wanted her stepdaughter Zawditu—Menelik's eldest child—to succeed her father. As a woman, Zawditu would not be able to reign in her own name. Her husband—who was Taytu's nephew—could be the regent while she would, in fact, govern. She would not have been Ethiopia's first woman ruler. Many powerful women had ruled as regents or consorts of emperors. But Menelik had other plans. On October 28, 1909, he suffered a massive stroke and named his eleven-year-old grandson, Lij Iyasu, as his successor.

Menelik died on December 12, 1913. Taytu Betul left her palace in Addis Ababa and retired to a **monastery** at Entotto Maryam. She died there of heart disease on February 11, 1918.

Haile Selassie

Born in 1892, Tafari Mekonnen helped to oust Lij Iyasu and to name Zawditu empress. She crowned him king, or ras, in 1928. In 1930, after Zawditu's death, Ras Tafari appointed himself emperor and became known by the name *Haile Selassie* ("Strength of the Trinity"). This photograph of him is from that year.

A group of Jamaicans became his followers, calling themselves Ras Tafarians. Their music, **reggae**, is now world famous. Haile Selassie was ousted by a coup in 1974 and died the following year. Since then, the country has been a republic.

In February 1917, after Lij Iyasu was forced out of power, Zawditu was finally crowned empress of Ethiopia. Her regent was not her husband but a grand nephew of Menelik, Ras Tafari Mekonnen. Under the name Haile Selassie, he became emperor in 1930, when Zawditu died.

Menelik II is remembered as a sovereign who vastly expanded his empire, who crushed Italy's attempt to turn Ethiopia into a colony, and who worked for the modernization of his country. He was greatly helped by his educated, politically aware, and open-minded wife. Together they kept their country unified and free, and opened it to a new age.

Nairobi, Kenya, in East Africa, has a population of more than 1.5 million.

Chapter Six

East Africa Today

With more than 250 million inhabitants, East Africa is the most populous part of the continent. East Africa has the youngest population, with 47 percent of the people under the age of fifteen.

East Africa is also the poorest and least stable area. Civil wars and wars of independence have taken a heavy toll in the past thirty years on Rwanda, Burundi, Ethiopia, Eritrea, Mozambique, Zimbabwe, and Sudan. As a result, the region has the largest number of refugees in the world.

Today all the countries are independent republics, except the islands of Réunion (near Madagascar) and Mayotte (in the Comoro Archipelago), which are French territories.

Many of the problems the kings and queens of yesterday faced continue to plague their successors. Ranavalona tried to keep the French at bay, but they seized her country. In 1947, France crushed a Malagasy rebellion, causing tens of thousands of deaths.

Yambio tried to protect his people and their land, but Sudan's political and social problems have persisted. A civil war between the North and the South, the Ethiopian intervention in the conflict, a border dispute with Egypt, and famines have plagued the country for the past twenty years.

After Italy took over Eritrea under Menelik II, the territory formed a short-lived federation with Ethiopia in the 1950s. It then fought a long war against Ethiopia and finally gained its independence in 1993. Nevertheless, skirmishes between the two countries continue.

But for all its problems, East Africa is also a place of fascinating cultures and ancient traditions, of extreme beauty and generous peoples who hope their future will be as extraordinary as their past.

Glossary

Beta Israel—a population also called *Falasha* or *Fellasha* whose origin is obscure. They say they are descendants of Jews who followed Menelik I when he left Jerusalem. Since 1984, most Falasha have settled in Israel.

emissary—a person sent to represent someone else

guerrilla warfare—actions carried out by small groups who can be civilians or members of an irregular army. Guerrilla groups are characterized by speed and mobility.

Indonesian—a native of Indonesia, a country made up of islands in South Asia

monastery—a community of persons who have made religious vows and live isolated from the rest of society

Malagasy—a native of Madagascar; a language spoken by the Malagasy people

nationalist—a member of a political party or group supporting national independence or strong national government

Nilotic—the Nilotic peoples, or Nilotes, are black Africans who live in certain areas of East Africa. They belong to several ethnic groups. Their name is associated with the Nile River area, where some live and where others come from.

Ottoman—another name for Turkey, or for a Turk—a native of Turkey

ras—a king in Ethiopia

regent—the person who rules when the sovereign is too young or sick

reggae—a popular type of music from Jamaica with a repetitive rhythm. It became known worldwide in the 1970s.

To Find Out More

Books

Blauer, Ettagale and Jason Lauré, *Madagascar*. Danbury, CT: Children's Press, 2000.

Bowden, Rob, Tony Binns, and Robert Bowden. *East Africa*. Austin, TX: Raintree Steck-Vaughn, 1998.

The Diagram Group. *The Peoples of East Africa*. New York: Facts on File, 1997.

Mann, Kenny. *Egypt, Kush, Aksum*. Parsippany, NJ: Dillon Press, 1997.

Newman, Shirlee P. *The African Slave Trade*. Danbury, CT: Franklin Watts, 2000.

Temko, Florence. *Traditional Crafts from Africa*. Minneapolis, MN: Lerner, 1996.

Wilson, Thomas. *City-States of the Swahili Coast*. Danbury, CT: Franklin Watts, 1999.

Organizations and Online Sites

Africa: The Art of a Continent: Eastern Africa
http://www.artnetweb.com/guggenheim/africa/east.html
Go to this nested page within the Guggenheim Museum site to learn more about the art of East Africa.

African Studies Association
Rutgers the State University of New Jersey
132 George Street – Douglass Campus
New Brunswick, NJ 08901-1400
This association sponsors research and the study of African subjects.

Ethiopian Embassy—Washington, D.C.
3506 International Drive N.W.
Washington, D.C., 20008
http://www.ethiopianembassy.org/
The embassy's website features fast facts, late-breaking news, and information about the government, economy, business, arts, and culture of Ethopia.

Madagascar
http://www.embassy.org/madagascar/
Learn about the currency, arts and crafts, official languages, points of interest, and weather of Madagascar by visiting the embassy's site.

The Museum of African American History
315 East Warren at Bush Street
Detroit, MI 48201
http://www.maah-detroit.org/
Learn about African and African-American history and culture by visiting this museum or its website.

Research Institute of African and African American
Diaspora Arts
12 Morley Street
Roxbury, MA 02119
This institute conducts research and provides educational programs on African culture.

A Note on Sources

The sources I consulted for this book included *The General History of Africa* (eight volumes), published by UNESCO and California University Press; *Encyclopedia of Africa South of the Sahara* (four volumes), John Middleton, ed.; *The Historical Dictionary of Madagascar* by Maureen Covell; *Madagascar: Conflicts and Authority in the Great Island* by Philip Allen; *Les souverains de Madagascar* by Françoise Raison-Jourde; *The Historical Dictionary of Sudan* by Carolyn Fluehr-Lobban; *The Azande: History and Political Institutions*; and *Zande Historical Texts* by Edward E. Evans-Pritchard; *A Modern History of the Sudan: From the Funj Sultanate to the Present Day* by Peter M. Holt; *Empress Taytu and Menelik II: Ethiopia 1883–1910* and *The Historical Dictionary of Ethiopia* by Chris Pouty; *The Life and Times of Menelik II* and *The Modern History of Ethiopia and the Horn of Africa* by Harold G. Marcus.

—*Sylviane Anna Diouf*

Index

Numbers in *italics* indicate illustrations.

About the Author

Sylviane Anna Diouf is the author of fiction and nonfiction books for adults and children and of numerous articles for international publications. She specializes in the history of Africa and of people of African origin.

Of Senegalese and French parentage, Ms. Diouf has lived in various African and European countries and in the United States. She has traveled in many parts of the world, and speaks several languages. She holds a doctorate from the University of Paris and lives in New York City with her son.